NEON Rock Art

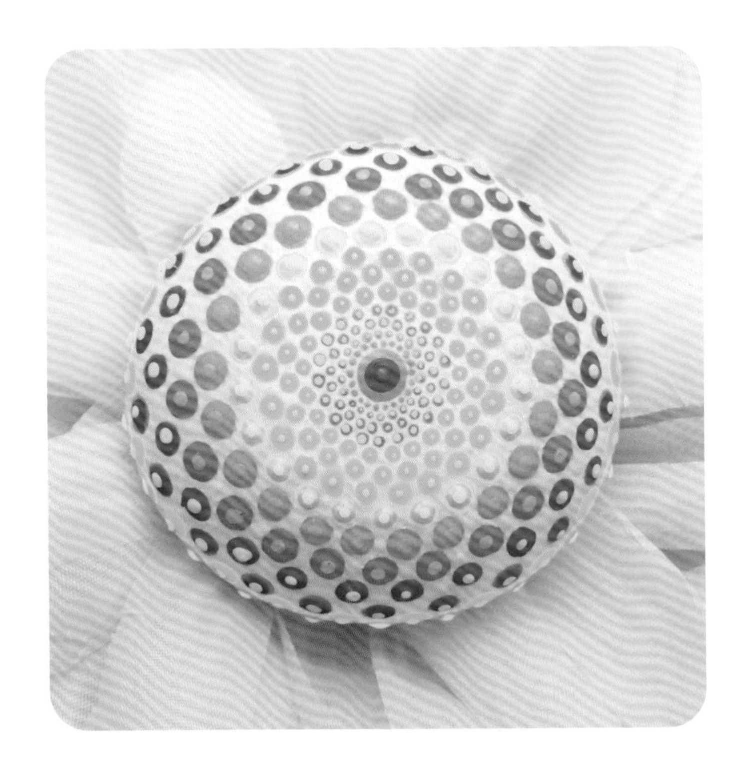

hinkler

About This Book

Rock art is one of the most ancient forms of artistic expression known to humans, and creating rock art is a hugely popular pastime. Using neon paint is a fantastic way to add a brilliant glow to your rocky works of art, highlighting and adding a fun, eye-catching element. Brighten up your bedroom with some dazzling neon pieces or light up a friend's day with a gorgeous gift.

There are 19 wonderful neon rock-painting activities in this book, including simple designs, cool geometric patterns and cute character pieces.

Contents

hinkler

Published by Hinkler Pty Ltd
45–55 Fairchild Street
Heatherton Victoria 3202 Australia
www.hinkler.com

Authors: Amanda Rogers and Katie Cameron
Cover design: Hinkler Studio

ISBN: 978 1 4889 5238 8

Printed and bound in China

Getting Started

ROCKS

The best rocks to paint on are smooth and relatively free of cracks or holes. Rocks that are too rough or pitted are not ideal because the paint will run and neat detailing is difficult to achieve. Rounded rocks make for nice symmetry, although you can paint on rocks of any shape. Keep in mind that the larger the rock, the longer it will generally take to complete.

If you are going to gather your own rocks (rock hunting is often half the fun!), smooth rocks are most often found along the shores of oceans and rivers. But if this is not an option or you want to save time, smooth rocks can be purchased from craft stores.

Be sure to thoroughly clean your rocks. Rinse off the bulk of any mud or sand outside (not down the kitchen drain!), and then give them a scrub in the sink with soap and water. Ensure that the rocks are free of any dust or debris and are completely dry before you begin.

IMPORTANT

Make sure it is OK to take the rocks from your area. Some places have regulations to protect the environment against things like erosion or risks to animal habitats, and sometimes it can also be culturally inappropriate. Ensure that you always ask permission if taking from private property.

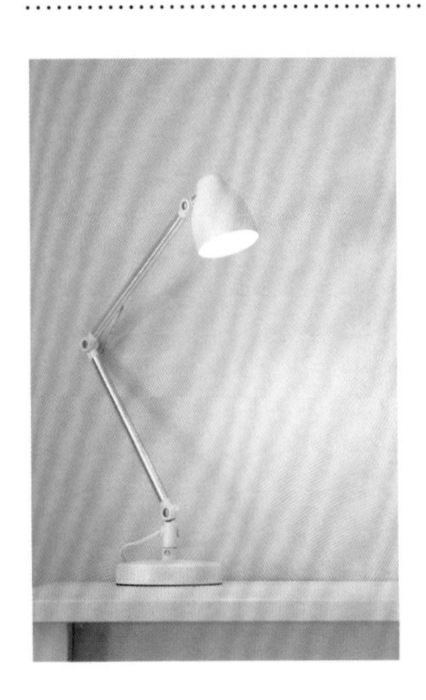

WORK SPACE

You will need a large, well-lit work station with enough space for you to paint and also have everything you need within arm's reach.

Your station should be high enough to maintain good posture, and be equipped with a comfortable chair. Painting these beautiful rocks can take a lot of time, so be aware of the time you're spending and try not to sit for too long! Be sure to get up, stretch and move around for ten minutes or so at least once an hour. Movement is good for your body's circulation and can also help you refocus.

To keep your work space neat and tidy, place a piece of cardboard or paper towel beneath your rock before you begin, and protect the remainder of your space with old newspaper. The cardboard helps to keep the underside of the rock clean and can also be helpful if you wish to move the rock to another area without needing to pick it up.

PAINTS

Regular craft or student acrylic paint works well for painting rocks. It is non-toxic, intermixable, fast drying and adheres well to a rock's surface. It's also cheap and easy to clean using a little soap and water. Most acrylic paint is easily intermixable. You can mix new colour combinations, darken shades with a little black or add white to lighten shades.

HANDY HINT

Have the paint colours you plan to use, or have been using, set aside. This comes in handy if you are mixing a new shade, picking up where you left off, or if you are applying a second coat. You don't want to apply a second coat in the wrong colour!

Be aware that neon acrylic colours are not alike across all brands. The intensity of the colour varies, as does the opacity. In general, neon colours are translucent. Neon paints require several coats to appear intense in colour and so that you cannot see what is beneath.

To save time and paint, prime your rock using white paint or a bright acrylic paint of the same colour as your neon paint (for example, regular lime green paint as a base coat under neon green paint). If you paint directly onto the rock, the dark surface of the rock will show through and the colour won't seem very neon. You can use this to your advantage: for instance, if you want a darker shade for the background or other detailing.

Allow neon paint to dry completely between coats or you may end up with streaks or uneven paint. Acrylic paint can take anywhere from 5–15 minutes to dry, depending on the thickness of the paint; though this is 'to the touch'. It can take 24 hours or more for acrylic craft paint to 'cure' to a point where it is completely dry.

Drying time is affected by many factors – how heavily it is applied, temperature, humidity, brand, colour and more. Don't touch the rock while it is drying; you risk leaving smudges or fingerprints. Even after the paint has dried, applying a finish can moisten it for a short time. The last thing you want at the final stage is a paint mishap, so hands off until you're sure the paint is firm!

HANDY HINT

If you store a lot of paints in a drawer or container where you cannot see each label, brush a dab of paint on the top of the lid. This way you can easily see which colour is which, and how it will look when dry. When you only have a few small dots to do, save paint by dipping your stick in the paint left in the cap after you shake the container, rather than pouring it onto a palette. Just don't forget to put the cap back on!

NOTES ABOUT NEON

Neon shades can be darkened with a little bit of black or lightened with a little white; however, you cannot make any new neon colours. Neon pigment is man-made and this brightness is generally limited to pink, orange, yellow, green, blue and red colours. You can intermix neon paint with regular acrylic paint to make some interesting new shades; the brightness will be muted but will still create some fun colours. Just don't expect to make a new neon!

Regular colours absorb light while neon absorbs and re-emits it, causing it to appear bright. Fluorescent colours are made using chemicals that cause fluorescence, meaning they will glow under a black or UV light.

GLOW-IN-THE-DARK PAINT

Glow-in-the-dark paint is a type of paint that you can see in the dark (obviously!) and is created using man-made chemicals. When you shine light on them, they absorb and store the light energy and then release it gradually. Glow paint won't glow forever without some recharging, of course! Just expose the paint to light (from a bright light bulb, a UV blacklight, or sunshine) to recharge it.

Glow paint tends to work best when it's applied over white or light-coloured backgrounds. Avoid uneven glow (caused by streaks or raised edges) by using less glow paint on your brush and applying thin coats, adding more as needed. Also, give your glow paint a little extra time to dry between coats: 10 to 15 minutes or more, depending on the thickness of the coat.

TOOLS

There are a few tools that are useful when painting rocks:

- Pencil and eraser – use these to sketch out your ideas and designs on paper beforehand. Light grey pencil markings can be used directly on the rock or dry paint, and an eraser can remove any marks, or you can simply paint over them.
- Drawing compass and ruler – you can use your eye to judge measurements like centre points for designs and base coats, but a ruler and compass are useful when forming new designs on paper. A compass may be difficult to use on some shapes of rocks; if this is the case, use your judgement to visually choose the centre spot.
- Paintbrushes – pointed brushes are best for fine detailing and lines, dotting and touch-ups. Use a larger sized round or flat brush when painting areas that need more coverage (i.e. base coats). Generally, brushes with shorter handles and shorter, firmer bristles work better to achieve precise detailing. Dot formation will vary with the amount of paint on the brush and the pressure you use. For larger dots, use a brush with larger bristles. It is important to keep your brushes in good condition with the bristles straight and together. Never let brushes dry with paint on them, and only dip them into the paint to about half the hair length so the paint doesn't get on the ferrule (the little metal piece that attaches the bristles to brush handle). Getting paint on the ferrule will inevitably result in spreading and frayed bristles, no matter how much you wash your paintbrush. Have a little cup of water at your work station so that you can quickly wash off paint and keep brushes moist before washing them thoroughly with soap and water.
- Paint or permanent-ink pens – use them to outline your design and to create extra-fine details that need to be all the same size, which can be very frustrating to achieve using paint and a brush!
- Dotting stylus – also known as a nail dotting tool or embosser, this looks similar to a pencil. It has a needle in one or both ends and a small round ball on the tip. This handy little device can be found at craft stores.
- Dotting tools – if you can't find a dotting stylus at your craft store, save money by using the pointed ends of household items. Think toothpicks, skewers, small dowels, unsharpened pencil ends, etc. These items allow greater precision and control when doing intricate dot work, and care is minimal as you do not have to clean them! You can allow the paint to dry on the sticks, which can layer and create new sizes for their ends; or you can pull off the dried paint and keep a small, pointed end.

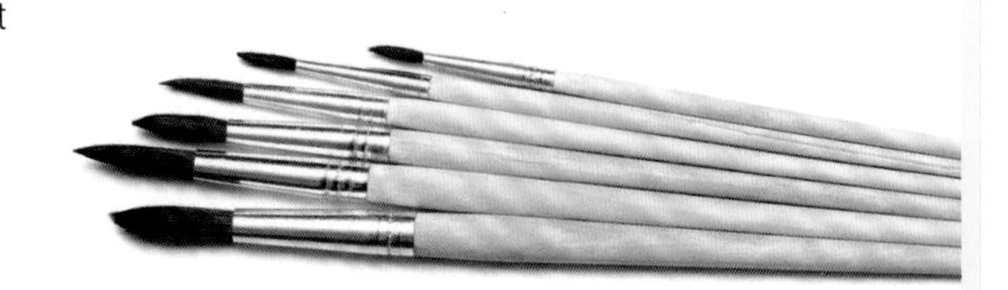

MAKING DOTS

To ensure accuracy when placing dots, hold the tool like a pencil and steady the rock with the other hand. Steady your aim by resting your hand, wrist or elbow against the desk or the rock itself.

Increasing the size of each dot from one row to the next is mostly a matter of having the right amount of paint on the right-sized tool. Usually, the smaller the point, the smaller the dot; you can use the small pointed end of a toothpick or the very tip of the longest bristle in a round paintbrush for your smallest dots.

HANDY HINT

If you're using dowels as dotting tools, you can sharpen them with a pencil sharpener to create a variety of dotting sizes.

The smallest dots do not require a lot of paint to make a well-formed circular dot. Too much paint and you could place a dot too large. You will need to wipe clean and re-dip the tool into the paint after each dot and use the same amount of pressure to maintain saturation and equal dot sizing.

When you want to go up a dot size, you can use the same sized dotting tool with slightly more paint and add just a bit more pressure while touching the stick to rock. If you do not wipe the paint from the stick before re-dipping, it will start to dry and accumulate, enlarging the end of the tool. A bigger tool end will give a bigger size dot.

To increase dot size, you can also use a larger tool. The diameter of the end of the tool you are using is a good indication of the size of the dot it will create and, of course, the more it is saturated with paint, the bigger the dot will be.

CLEAR FINISH

Most craft stores stock affordable clear, gloss or matte acrylic finishes that will make your colours appear brighter and seal them in place longer. It will also protect against fading, and make your rocks resistant to water and weather conditions. The spray-on type is preferable to the brush-on type, as this is quick and easy, and adheres to all parts of the rock in a uniform, even manner.

Always wait until your rock is complete, the paint is completely dry and hard, and the rock is free of any dust or unwanted particles before spraying the protective finish in a well-ventilated room or outside. Allow at least a day for the finish to dry, then apply a second coat and allow it to dry again. As with paint, avoid touching your rock while the finish is drying to ensure the coating hardens smoothly.

If you do not wish to use a protective finish, try using acrylic 'outdoor' paints, which are designed with a finish built in. These outdoor craft paints are more durable than regular acrylic paints; however, they cost more, and are not as durable as a separate finishing coat.

Some paint or permanent-ink pens can bleed or smear when finish is applied. If you are using these pens, make sure you test how they react to a finish before you apply the finish to your rock. To do this, use your pen on some dry white paint on the underside of a rock. Ensure the paint is dry before applying a clear finish to see the result. If the ink reacts with the finish, it will blur into the white paint. You might want to either skip the finish or apply it first and go back to add in details over top. This way you won't ruin your hard work at the final stage!

FIXING MISTAKES AND OTHER TIPS AND TRICKS

Here are a few other little tips that I'd like to share before you start your neon rock-painting journey.

PATIENCE

Painted rocks can take many hours, if not days, to complete. Patience is key. If you rush, you may make mistakes that could have been avoided. That being said, don't worry too much about tiny imperfections. In the grand scheme of things, they often go unnoticed in all the other details.

DOT FIX

Dropped an uneven dot or made one so big it ran into the others? Depending on where and when in the process this happens, you may be able to wipe the paint away using some water and a brush, or scrape the mistake off with a stick or some fine sandpaper. It is safer to allow the area (if not the entire rock) to dry before you try to fix mistakes. Clear away any flakes before repainting the area with the same colour as the underlying coat. Allow the new paint to dry and reapply your dot. It's like it never happened!

ACRYLIC 'ERASER'

The good thing about acrylic paint is that it is very thick – you can use it to paint over a mistake without the original paint showing through. The base colour is your friend! Use it as an 'eraser' for small mistakes. Don't like the dot colour you have chosen? Dot right over the top of it!

HANDY HINT

Speed up drying time between coats by using a hair dryer on a low setting.

WONKY DESIGN

If you didn't quite start in the middle and your design is off centre, use more base paint to even out the circle, thus centring your design. If you have messed up more than it's worth taking the time to fix, scrub off the paint using soap and water. It is just a rock, after all!

CLEAR FINISH SPRAY

After pencilling your design onto a rock or on the base coat, spray the rock with a coat of clear finish and allow it to dry before beginning to paint. This prevents the pencil marks or base paint from mixing into the paint of the design, especially when many brush strokes are involved.

BEFORE YOU BEGIN

Here are a few tips before you start your rock-painting journey.

PLAN AHEAD

Sketch out your design idea before you start. Trace the shape of your rock onto a piece of paper so you can get an idea what will fit on your 'canvas'. Use a ruler and drawing compass to practise making circles and other geometric shapes. It is helpful to get the hang of a pattern on paper before it's set on rock.

DOT PRACTICE

Practise, practise, practise! Precision with dots takes a steady hand and knowing how to place the brush or stick with just the right pressure. Dip your tool into the paint often to leave a thick, nicely saturated dot. This means that your dot is less likely to need a second coat of paint, and you are less likely to make a mistake. Try out different styles of dot art and practise making shapes and patterns. Before starting, use the dotting tool to do a test dot on some paper to get a feel for how the paint will transfer and what pressure is needed for an evenly shaped circular dot.

HANDY HINT

If you can't find the perfect rock for the design you want to paint, try forming your own 'rocks' using store-bought polymer clay.

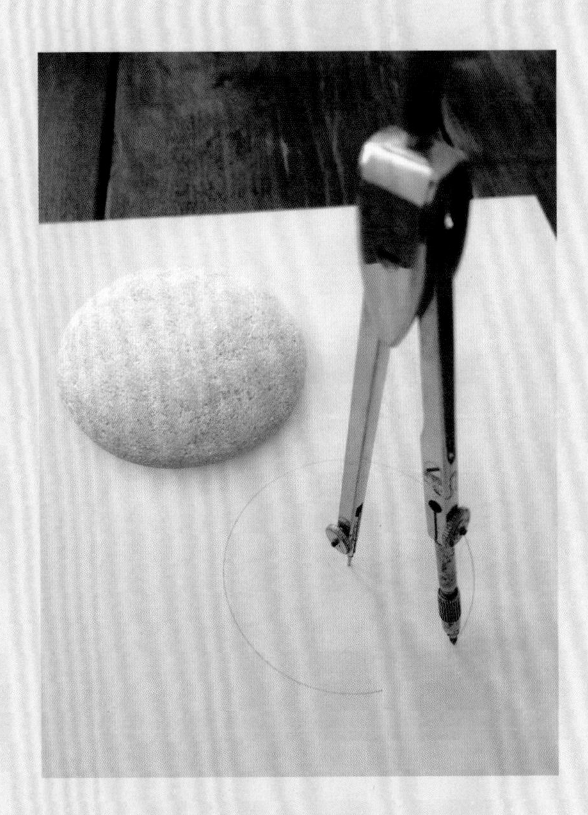

BRUSH-STROKE PRACTICE

Brushes come in different sizes and shapes to create different paint strokes. Use a large flat brush to cover big areas and a small, round brush for details and outlines. Paint large areas or backgrounds first. Start with mid to bright colours and then add dark colours.

Dot Mandala

You will be seeing spots, or should I say dots, after painting this neon beauty!

YOU WILL NEED:

- Small, round rock
- Pencil
- Paint: neon pink, yellow, green
- Paintbrush
- Dotting tool
- Toothpicks
- Protective finish

Mark the centre of the rock with a pencil.

HANDY HINT

Cut a circle out of paper the size of the rock and fold it in half twice. Use a toothpick to make a tiny hole in the middle where the two folds cross and use this to find the centre of the rock.

Use a toothpick to make a row of pink dots around the centre dot. Use a dotting tool to make two more pink rows and then two yellow rows. Make each row of dots fit in the spaces between the dots in the previous row, not in line with them.

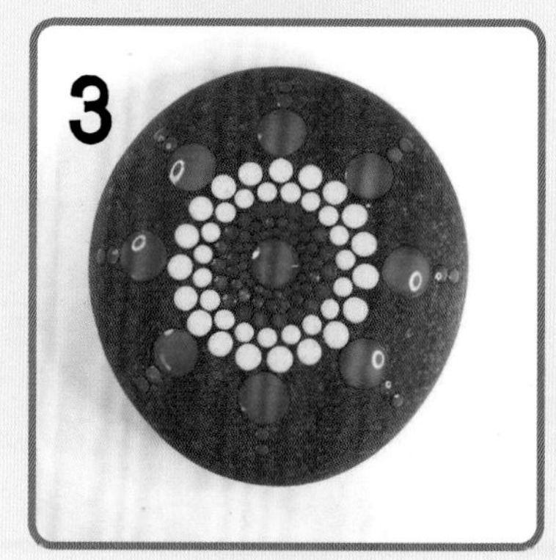

Use a dotting tool to make four neon pink dots at the north, south, east and west points of the mandala. Then place a pink dot between each of those dots so there are eight equally spaced dots as shown. Use the toothpick to make two dots on the outer edge of the larger dots.

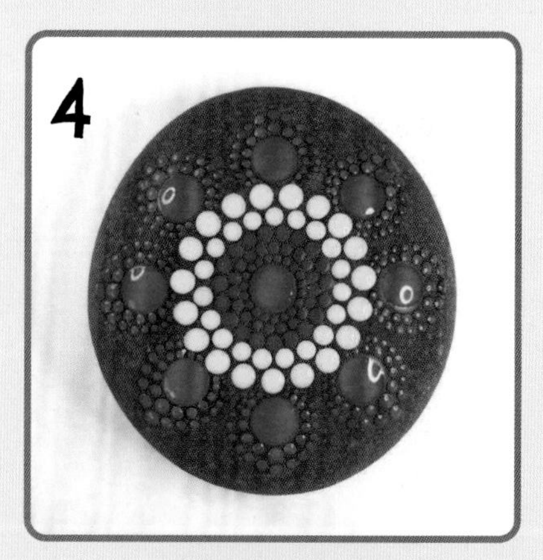

Use the toothpick to make some rows of neon pink dots. Place a dot next to one of the small dots you just made and make a line of dots without getting more paint. Get a new drop of paint for each new row. By using the same drop of paint for each line, the dots will naturally get smaller as you go.

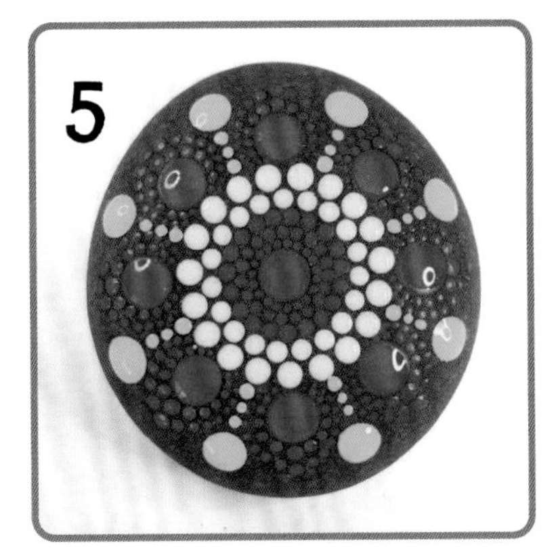

Fill in the remaining space with neon green dots. Use the toothpick to make three dots in between the lines of dots, followed by a larger dot with the dotting tool.

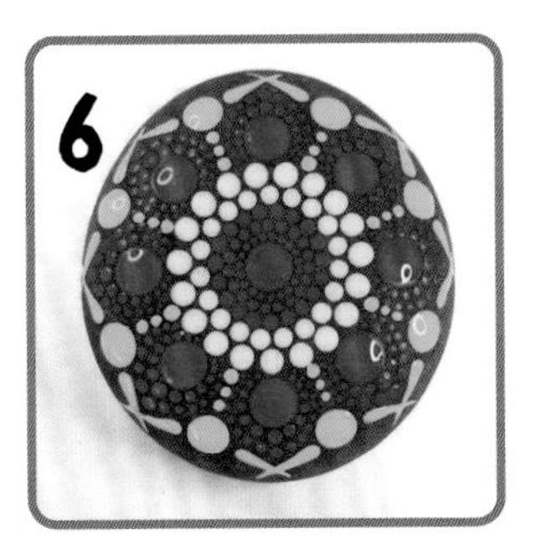

The edges of the rock will be finished with swipes using a brush and green neon paint. Start the swipe next to each large green dot and drag the swipe out to a point. Make the two swipes cross over each other.

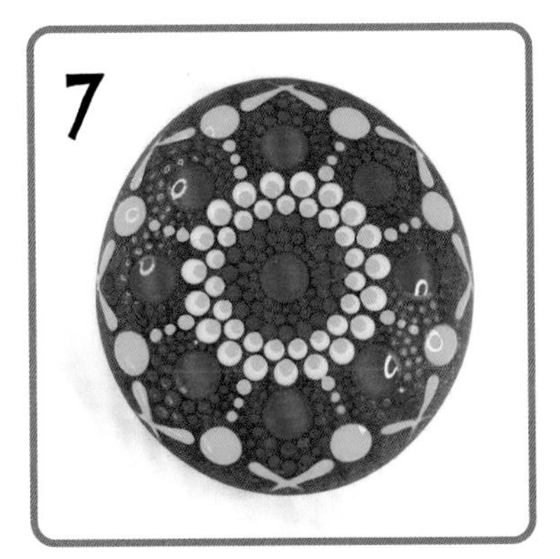

Use the toothpick to put green dots on top of the yellow dots. Make the dots off centre, towards the middle of the mandala, and make sure you don't cover the entire yellow dot.

HANDY HINT

Let the dots dry completely before putting on the top dots.

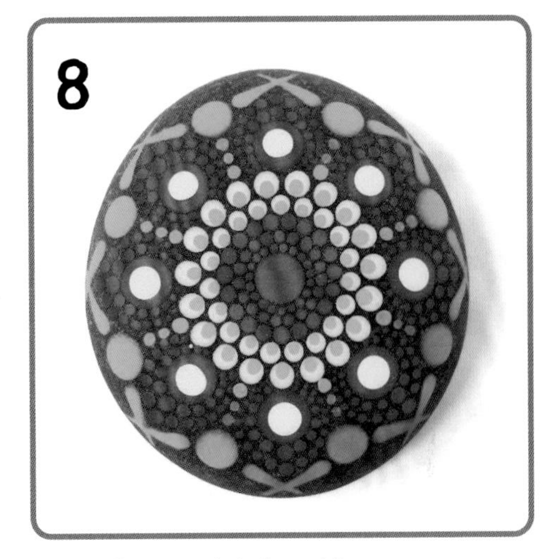

Finish the mandala by adding yellow top dots on the large pink dots with a dotting tool. Once dry, add protective finish.

Retro Heart

Prepare to have so much fun painting this neon rock your heart might skip a beat!

YOU WILL NEED:

- Small, oval-shaped rock
- Pencil
- Paint: black, white; neon pink, yellow, green
- Paintbrush
- Dotting tool
- Protective finish

Paint the base coat black and once dry, draw a heart that covers the top surface of the rock with the pencil.

HANDY HINT

Use a ruler to make sure your horizontal lines are extra straight.

Draw lines horizontally on the heart with the pencil.

Paint the lines white.

Use the dotting tool to make dots with white paint all the way around the outside of the rock. Hold the tool parallel to the rock and lift the tool just before it touches the rock to prevent air bubbles.

Paint over the white lines with the pink, yellow and green neon paints.

HANDY HINT

Allow the lines to dry before painting the dots. This way, you can hold the rock in the centre while painting the dots around the edge.

Use the dotting tool to paint over the white dots with the neon paints. Wait until your paint is completely dry, then use your protective coating and admire your creation!

We Rock!

Rock out painting this colourful neon rock!

YOU WILL NEED:

- Larger rock
- Pencil
- Paint: black, white; neon yellow, pink, green
- Paintbrush
- Dotting tool
- Protective finish
- Stencil (optional)

1. Cover the rock with a black paint base coat.

2. Draw the text on the rock using a pencil and then paint over it with white paint.

3. Draw a triangle border around the text and three decorative triangles as shown, and cover them with white paint.

HANDY HINT

If you find it tricky to draw the letters freehand, try using a stencil instead.

4. Use a dotting tool and finish the edge of the rock with lines of white dots. Make the dots get smaller on each line.

Paint over the letters with pink neon paint.

Paint over the large triangle with the yellow neon paint. If you get some of the yellow on the black paint, don't worry. You can paint over it with black paint once it's dry.

Now cover the three white triangles with the yellow, pink and green neon paints.

Use the very tip of the brush to add a white line down the centre of the neon lines and on the dots to simulate neon lights glowing. Cover the rock with protective finish and rock on!

Ice-Cream Rock

Cool down with this yummy ice-cream neon sign rock!

YOU WILL NEED:

- Small, oval-shaped rock
- Pencil
- Paint: black, white; neon yellow, pink, orange, green
- Paintbrush: small, large
- Dotting tool: small
- Protective finish

Use the large brush to paint the rock with a black base coat.

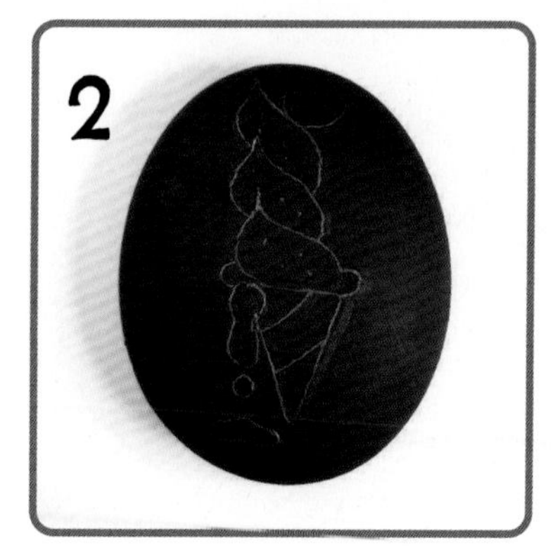

Draw the ice-cream onto the rock with the pencil.

HANDY HINT

Using a base layer of white paint makes the neon paint pop.

Use the small brush to paint the ice-cream with white paint.

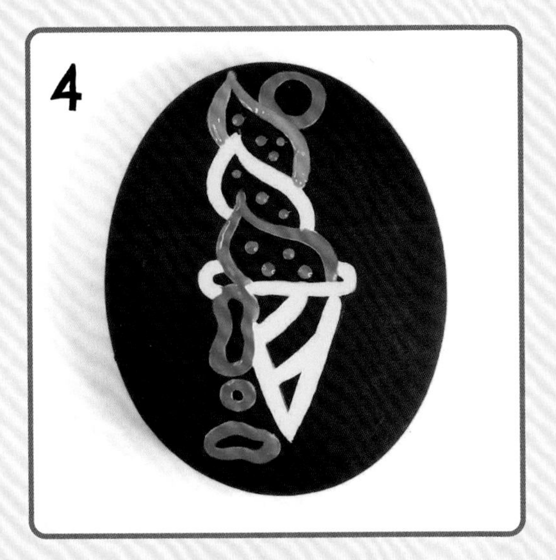

Wait for the white paint to dry completely and paint over it with the yellow, pink and orange neon paints. If you make a mistake and get neon paint on the black base coat, wait for it to dry and paint over it again with black to redefine the edges!

Use the small dotting tool to make flowers with a small dot in the centre and five large petal dots around it. First, make them using white paint, then after they dry, cover the petals with green neon paint.

Paint a thin white line down the centre of the neon lines of the ice-cream to simulate neon lights glowing. Use the small dotting tool to add black dots to the flower petals to give them more depth. Once the paint dries, protect with coating and your ice-cream cravings shall be satisfied!

Line Mandala

Get your Zen on painting this meditative lotus flower rock.

YOU WILL NEED:

- Small, round rock
- Pencil
- Paint: white; neon yellow, pink, green, blue, orange
- Paintbrush: small, large
- Dotting tool: small, large
- Toothpicks
- Protective finish

Use the large brush to paint the rock with a white base coat.

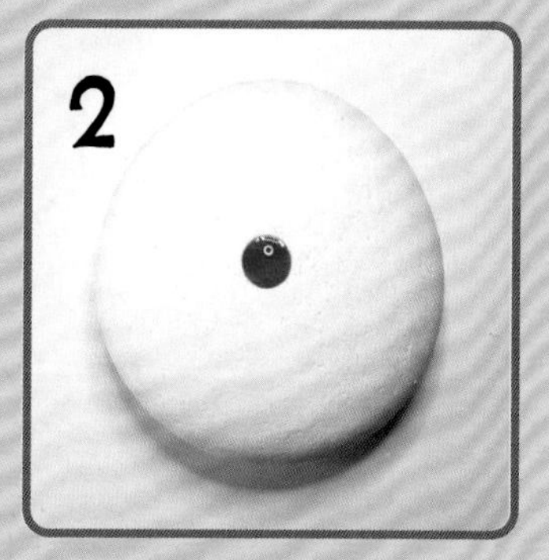

Mark the centre of the rock with a pencil and use the large dotting tool to make a dot with pink neon paint.

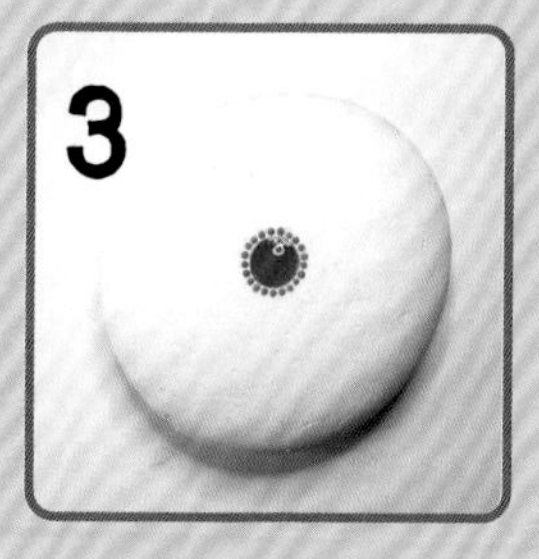

HANDY HINT

Place the dotting tool in a vertical position to make sure the dots are round and not oval.

Use a toothpick to make a row of small orange neon dots around the centre dot. Use the same amount of paint for each dot to ensure they are the same size and height so they dry evenly.

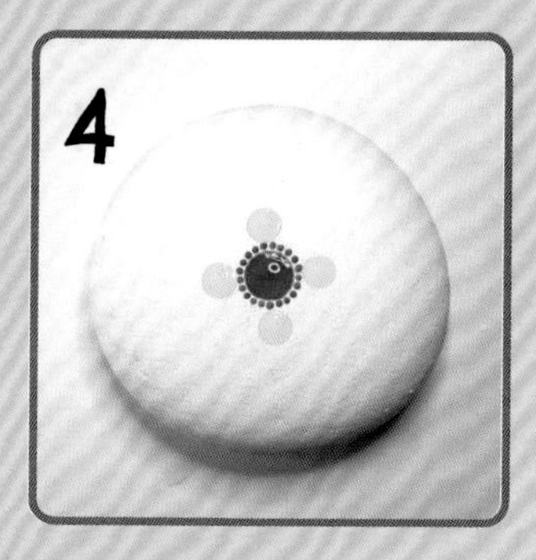

Use the large dotting tool to make four yellow neon dots as shown. When using larger tools, lift the tool just before it touches the rock to prevent air bubbles. If this does happen, let it dry, paint over it with the base paint and try again.

Use the small brush to make two green lines around each of the yellow dots. Make the lines meet at the end at a point.

Use a toothpick to make two small pink dots between each line and use the large dotting tool to make a large orange dot.

Use the small brush to make two blue lines around the large orange dots. Use a toothpick to make pink dots along the lines. Use one drop of paint for each line of dots and the dots will naturally get smaller as you go. Use the brush again to make two yellow lines around the pink dots.

Make a large pink dot in each space. Make an orange line and green dots as in step 7, and then two more blue and yellow lines.

Make blue dots and green lines to fill up the remaining space.

Put white dots on top of the larger dots. Make these smaller dots off-centre on the base dots, towards the middle of the mandala. Add protective coating once the dots dry, and find a place for your new lotus mandala rock!

Rainbow Rock

Bring a little colour into your life with this bright, fun rainbow rock.

YOU WILL NEED:

- Small, oval-shaped rock
- Pencil
- Paint: black, white; neon yellow, blue, green, orange, pink
- Paintbrush: small, large
- Protective finish

1

Use the large brush to cover the rock with a black paint base coat. Let it dry, then use the pencil to draw a cloud and a rainbow with two stars.

HANDY HINT

Practise drawing your rainbow design on a piece of paper first.

2

Cover the pencil lines with white paint using the small brush.

3

Paint over the stars and the third line down with yellow neon paint.

Paint over the first line with pink neon paint and the second line with orange.

Paint the final line with green neon paint.

Paint the cloud blue!

Once the paint is completely dry, paint a fine white line down the centre of each line in the rainbow to simulate a glow of neon lights. Once the rock is dry, use your protective coating. When the sun hits this rainbow, it will really stand out!

Palm Trees

Get ready to paint these 'tree'mendous palm trees!

YOU WILL NEED:

- Small, round rock
- Pencil
- Paint: blue, white; neon yellow, green, orange
- Paintbrush: small, large
- Dotting tool: small, large
- Protective finish

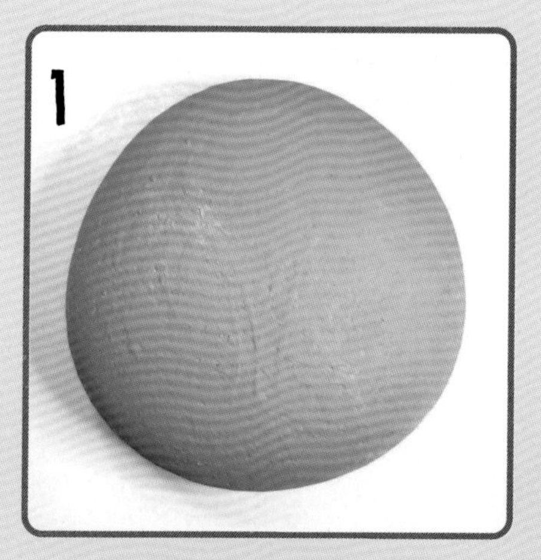

Use the large brush to paint the rock with a blue base coat.

Draw the palm-trees image with a pencil and use the small brush to cover it with white paint.

Once the white paint dries, cover the trunks of the trees and the outer circle with yellow neon paint.

Cover the tops of the trees with green neon paint using the small brush. Cover the water lines with the blue paint.

HANDY HINT

If the neon paint gets on the blue base coat, simply paint over it with blue paint when you are finished!

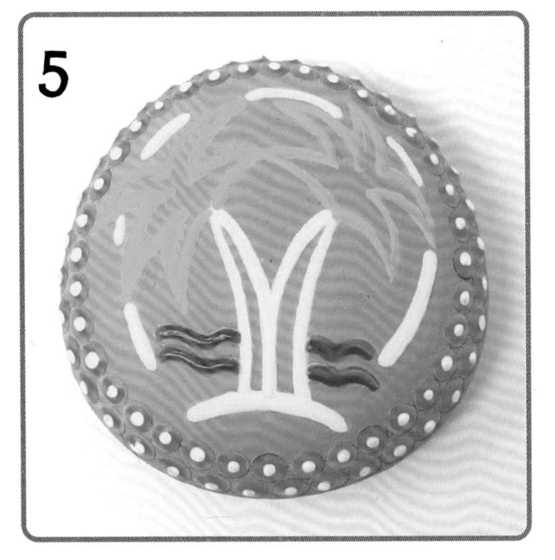

Draw a circle around the outside of the image. Use the large dotting tool to cover the circle with a row of orange dots and then make a second row of orange dots outside of the first line. Once the dots completely dry, use the small dotting tool to put yellow dots in the centre of the orange dots.

Once the green, yellow and blue paint is dry, use the small brush to paint a thin white line down the centre of each of the neon lines. This will make it look like a glowing neon sign! Let this one dry overnight before adding your protective coating.

A Cherry Sweet Rock

Let's have some fun with this neon rock with a cherry on top!

YOU WILL NEED:

- Small, round rock
- Pencil
- Paint: black, white; neon pink, green, yellow
- Paintbrush: small, large, fine tip
- Dotting tool: small, large
- Protective finish

Use the large brush to make a circle with the black paint in the centre of the rock leaving the edges of the rock showing.

Draw a set of cherries on the black circle with your pencil.

HANDY HINT

Neon paint is not highly pigmented so it takes 2-3 coats of neon to make it bright and vibrant.

Use the small brush and paint over the lines with the pink and green neon paints.

Use the small brush and paint a yellow ring around the outside of the black circle.

Time to make some dots! Use the large dotting tool and dip it in the pink neon paint. Hold the tool vertical and press down on the rock. Lift the tool just before it touches the rock to prevent air bubbles. Leave a small space between each of the dots.

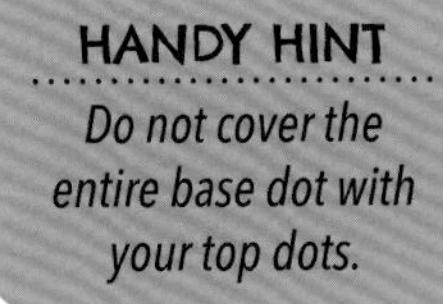

Use the small brush with green neon paint. Paint a line around either side of the dots and make the lines meet at the end. If you slowly lift the brush as you make the line, it will make it thick at the beginning and thin with a nice point at the end.

Use the small dotting tool and place a small white dot on top of each of the pink dots. Use the fine-tip brush and paint a thin white line on the cherries and the yellow circle as shown. This will simulate the glow of neon lights! Protect with coating and stand back and admire your neon cherries!

X Marks The Dot

Use this simple design to practise your dotting skills. Feeling creative? Try replacing the dots with little hearts or tiny crosses!

YOU WILL NEED:

- Oval-shaped rock
- Pencil
- Ruler (optional)
- Dotting tool: small
- Paintbrushes: small, large
- Paint: white; neon purple, green, yellow, orange, pink
- Protective finish

Begin with a dotted X in the centre of the rock using a dotting tool and neon purple paint. Make the centre dot larger than the four dots around it.

HANDY HINT

This design looks great on a light-coloured rock, or you can use a dark base coat to contrast with the bright neon paint.

Keep making dots out from either side of the X to form a horizontal line of dots across the middle of your rock.

Keep making dots out from the top and bottom of the X to form a vertical line of dots, sectioning your rock into four quarters.

Use white paint to add rows of dots either side of your purple dots.

HANDY HINT

It is important to keep turning the rock as you paint so that you can view the design as either an X or a +. This helps with estimating where to place new dots.

Once the white paint has dried, paint over the white dots with neon green paint. The white paint underneath will help the neon paint stand out.

Repeat steps 4 and 5 with neon yellow then neon orange paint.

Using white paint and a small paintbrush, add hearts in the empty spaces inside the rows of orange dots.

Allow the white paint to dry and paint the hearts in neon pink. Allow the whole design to dry, then apply a second coat (or more) to the dots if needed. Always leave it to dry completely between coats.

Once dry, cover your rock with protective finish.

Triangled

Have fun with this optical illusion design. As you paint this rock, all kinds of shapes and patterns begin to emerge, depending on how you look at it.

YOU WILL NEED:

- Rock
- Masking tape
- Ruler
- Craft blade
- Cutting board
- Paintbrushes: small, large
- Paint: grey, white, blue, purple; neon pink, yellow, green, orange
- Protective finish

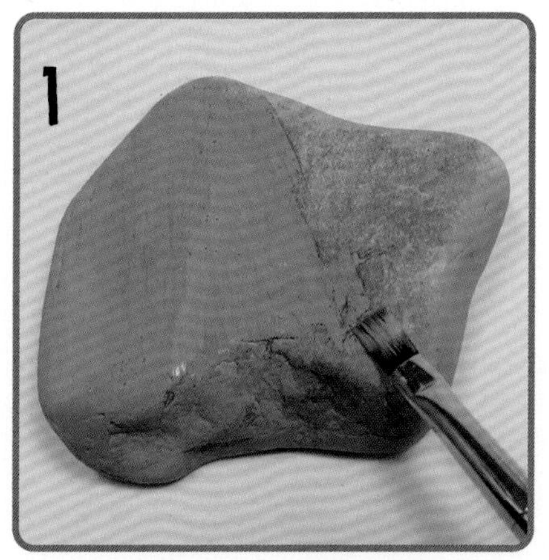

First, cover your rock with a grey base coat using a large round or flat brush.

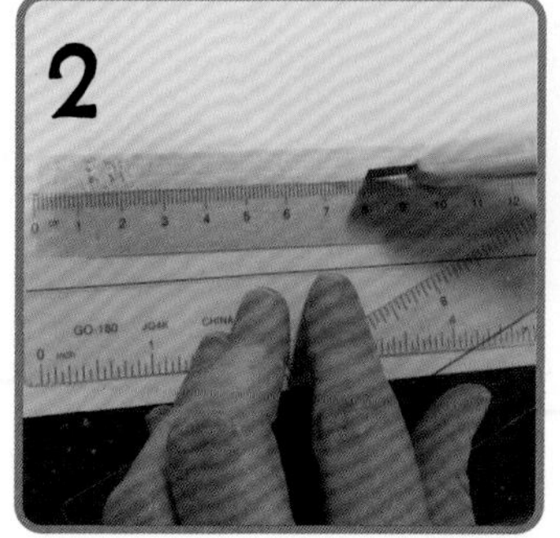

Layer 6–8 pieces of masking tape on top of one another. Ask an adult to help you cut the tape into thin strips.

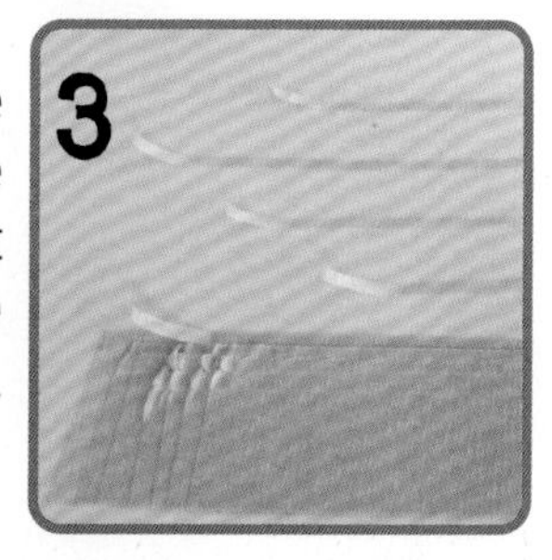

When you are finished, peel the tape layers apart and separate your strips.

Next, lay a row of strips across the rock horizontally, about 1 cm (0.4 in) apart. Lay another row of diagonal strips, running from top-left to bottom-right. Then, lay a second row of diagonal strips, running in the opposite direction.

Use a large brush or a sponge to cover the top of the rock with white paint.

When the white paint is completely dry, use whatever colours you like to paint the triangles.

Now comes the fun part! Carefully peel off the tape to reveal your triangle design. Go strip by strip, removing the top layer first.

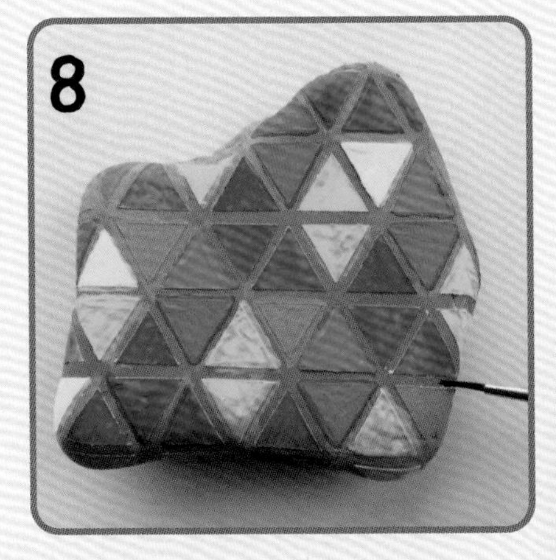

Touch up any messy lines with paint and a small brush. Allow to dry and then evenly coat with 1–2 coats of protective finish.

HANDY HINT

Get creative with your colours! Try a mix of both neon and regular colours, or just two or three neon colours throughout.

Infinity Rocks

Get ready to create your very own hand-held galaxy. Don't get dizzy with all those dots!

YOU WILL NEED:

- Round rock
- Dotting tools: small, medium, large
- Paintbrushes: large
- Paint: black, white, light blue, mid-blue, dark blue neon purple, pink, yellow, blue
- Protective finish

HANDY HINT

Practise this dot design on paper beforehand so you get the hang of how it works.

Use a large brush to paint a black base coat. Allow to dry.

Use a dotting tool and white paint to add a large dot to the centre of your rock. Use a small dotting tool or a toothpick to surround the large dot with tiny dots.

Keep adding rings of dots, making each new ring of dots slightly bigger than the last.

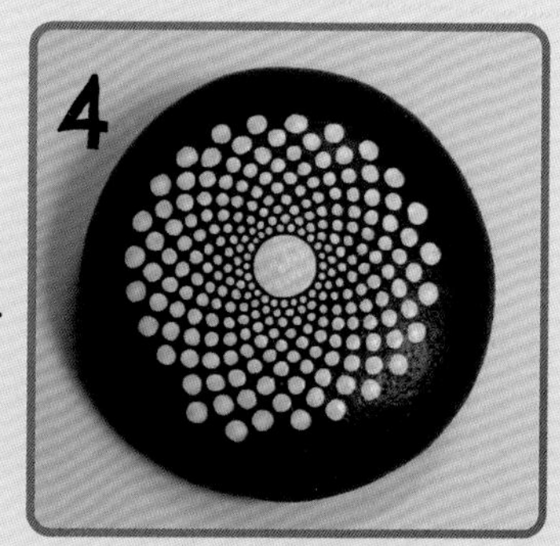

Continue adding rings of dots, turning the rock as you go.

Continue adding rings of dots until you have covered the rock right to the edge.

It's time to add colour! Start by painting over the smallest dots around the large centre dot. Begin with purple, followed by light blue, mid-blue and dark blue in that order. Repeat the colour pattern until the ring is complete.

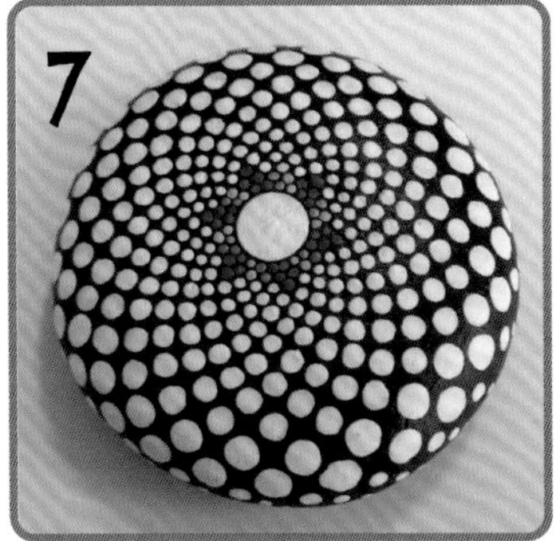

For the next ring, move the colour pattern one dot over. Beginning again with purple, place the dot above and to the right of the same colour dot in the ring before it. Continue to paint the colours in the same order for 3–4 rings. Now you should be able to see each colour curving away from the centre.

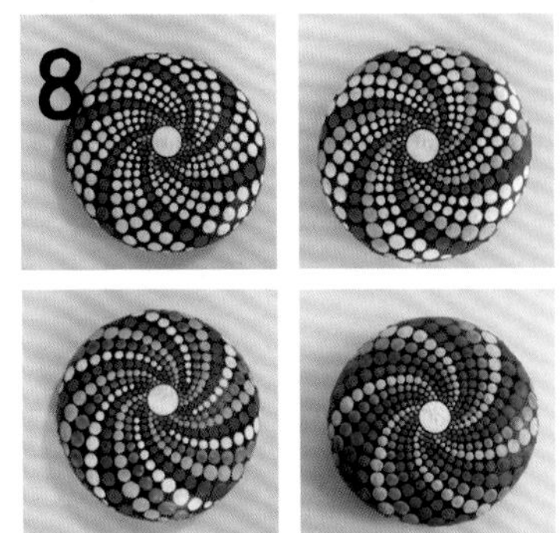

Finish each colour one at a time, row by row. For example, all purple dots, then all light blue dots, and so on.

Paint the centre dot dark blue and go over the blue and purple dots with a slightly lighter colour. Add a tiny dot of lighter colours to each of the dots.

To finish, add some bright stars to this galaxy. Use your small dotting tool to make tiny neon yellow dots in all the little spaces around each dot.

Add a light-blue dot on top of the centre dot, leave to dry and then coat with protective finish.

Owl Friend

Tired of dotting? Turn a plain rock into a little owl pal. It'll be a hoot!

YOU WILL NEED:

- Oval-shaped rock
- Pencil
- Paintbrushes: small, large
- Thin brush or black paint pen
- Paint: white, orange, black; neon orange, yellow, pink, blue, green, purple
- Protective finish

HANDY HINT

Practise your owl design on paper before you start.

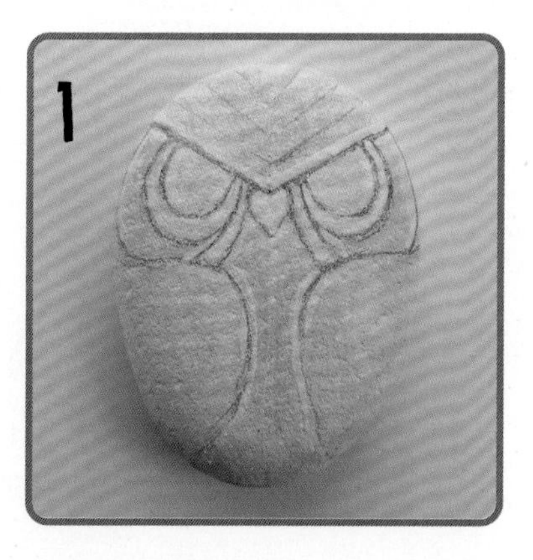

Use a large brush to prime your rock with 1–2 coats of white paint. Allow to dry. Lightly pencil the main outline of the owl on the rock, copying the lines in the image.

Paint the front area between the wings with neon orange paint. Use a small brush to paint the centre of the eye black with a neon yellow ring around it.

Use a thin brush and black paint to go over any pencil outlines. Use white paint to even out lines and fix any mistakes. Dry for 20 minutes or until the paint is completely dry.

Paint the V-shaped lines at the top of the owl's head neon pink, neon yellow and neon blue. Then, paint the beak and middle of the body neon orange. Finally, paint the wings neon purple, neon yellow and neon green in shaped sections as shown.

Paint the inside section around the eyes neon orange, pink and purple. Paint the next ring neon green, neon blue and neon orange. The outer spaces to the side of the rock are painted neon green, blue, pink and yellow.

When the paint has completely dried, use a small round brush and white paint to add diamond shapes to the front, and tiny dots to the wings and brow. Finally, add a white V-shape at the very top of the owl's head. Leave to dry.

Use a small brush and neon paint to paint the white details. Then, use black paint or a thin black pen to add arrow shapes to the green parts of the wings. Finally, add rows of dots to the V shapes at the top of the owl's head.

Apply 1–2 coats of protective finish and leave to dry for 24 hours.

New Bass Friend

Bring a bit of underwater wonder to dry land with this bright little fish friend. Play with the colour combinations and have fun!

YOU WILL NEED:

- Rock
- Pencil and paper
- Dotting tools: small, medium, large
- Paintbrushes: small, large
- Thin brush or black paint pen
- Paint: white, black; neon pink, yellow, purple, orange, blue, green
- Protective finish

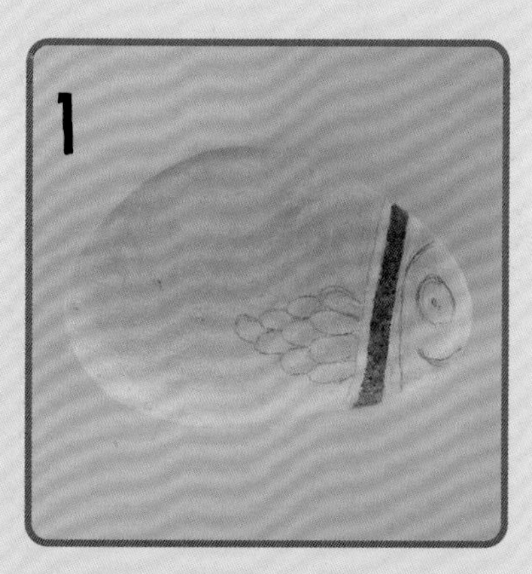

Paint the rock with a white base coat and allow to dry. Use a pencil to lightly draw in the head, face and fin as shown.

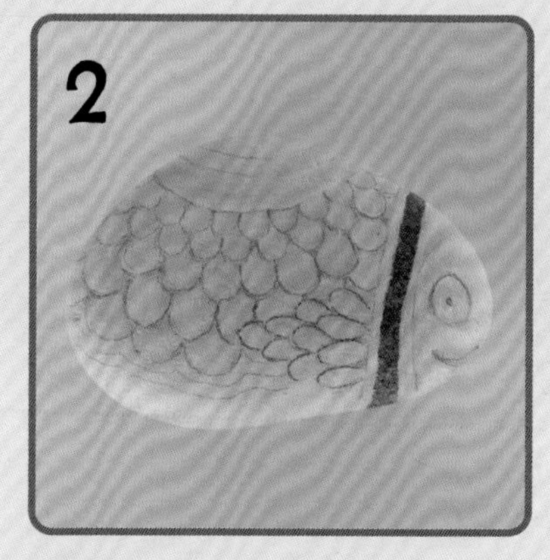

Continue drawing in the remaining scales, using U shapes in different sizes. Add three curved lines at the top.

Use a small brush and neon purple, pink and yellow paint to paint everything except the scales.

HANDY HINT

If you find it tricky to paint the fine black details with a brush, try using a fine-tipped permanent marker.

4

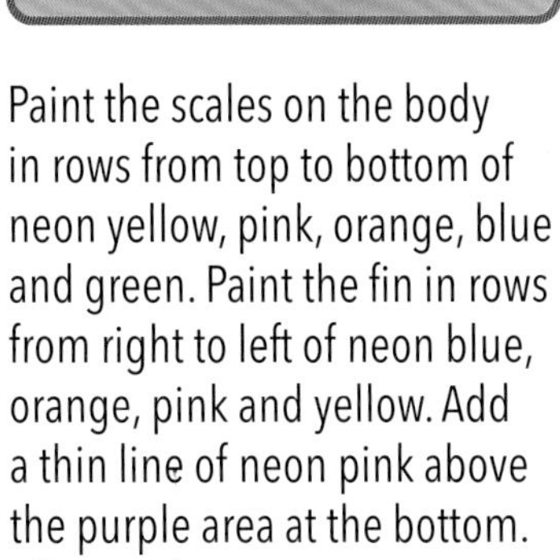

Paint the scales on the body in rows from top to bottom of neon yellow, pink, orange, blue and green. Paint the fin in rows from right to left of neon blue, orange, pink and yellow. Add a thin line of neon pink above the purple area at the bottom. Allow to dry.

5

Use a dotting tool and white, neon pink, neon blue and neon yellow paint to add dotted details. Use a thin brush and black paint to add line and dot details to the scales as shown.

6

Add more dots to the top of the fish, allow to dry and then apply one or two coats of protective finish.

HANDY HINT

Once your finished fish is completely dry, why not challenge yourself and paint the other side of the rock, too!

Rock Garden

Make your very own rock garden. These pretty posies are the perfect flower: they stay in bloom all year!

YOU WILL NEED:

- Oval-shaped rock
- Pencil
- Dotting tools: small, medium, large
- Paintbrushes: small, large
- Thin brush or white and black paint pens (both optional)
- Paint: white, black, red, light pink; neon pink, yellow
- Protective finish

Paint a large white circle on your rock and allow to dry. Use a pencil to lightly draw in the flower design as shown.

Fill the flower shape with black paint and allow to dry. Use a pencil to add another ring of petals around the black shape, about twice the size of the first row of petals. Add another, larger row of petals and then fill both rows with white paint.

Use a small brush and black paint (or a permanent marker) to go over the pencil lines. Leave a thin outline of white around the outside of the flower.

Add a small white dot to the centre of the black shape and then surround it with a ring of red paint. Once dry, add white dots to the red ring.

Use a thin brush and white paint to add lots of thin white lines extending out from the red circle. Add a tiny white dot on the end of each thin line.

Paint the middle row of petals with neon pink paint, leaving a small space of white outline between the pink paint and the petals of the ring before. Once dry, add stripes to the outer ring of petals with light pink paint.

Once dry, use a small brush or dotting tool to add in extra details. Try adding dots and lines to the pink petals.

HANDY HINT

If you're adding multiple coats of neon paint, make sure you allow each coat to dry before adding the next.

When all paint is dry, spray with 1–2 coats of protective finish and leave it to dry overnight.

Balance Cats

Create a happy balance with this adorable pair of intertwined kitties! This rock makes a perfect little gift for the cat lovers in your life.

YOU WILL NEED:

- Round rock
- Pencil
- Drawing compass
- Paint: white, black, and glow paint
- Paintbrushes: small, large
- Protective finish

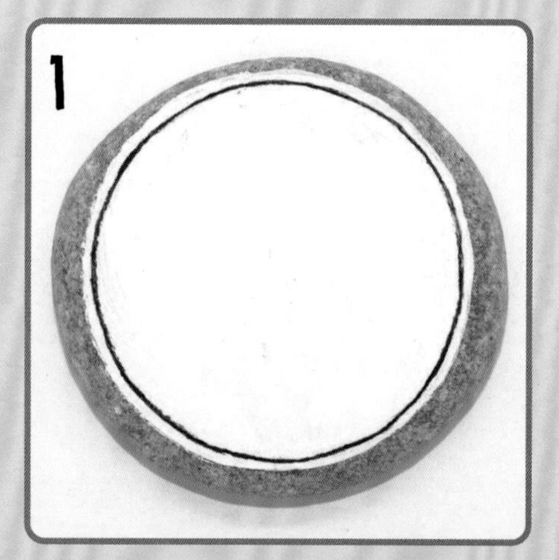

Using a pencil and compass, draw a circle on your rock. Fill in the circle with white paint and allow to dry. Draw another, slightly smaller circle just inside the first. Paint over the border of the smaller circle with a thin black line.

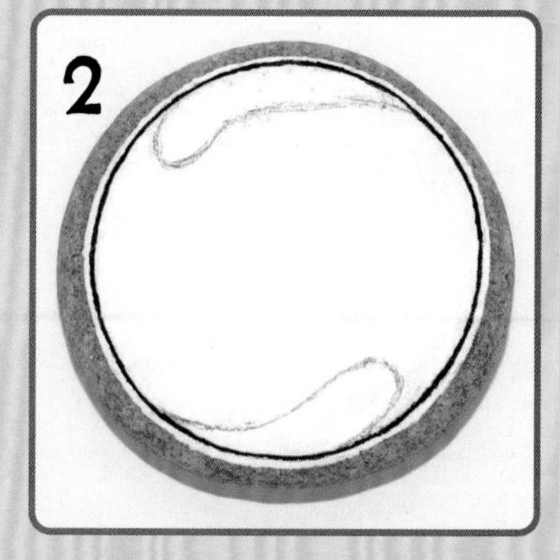

Once dry, use a pencil to lightly draw in the beginning of the design as shown.

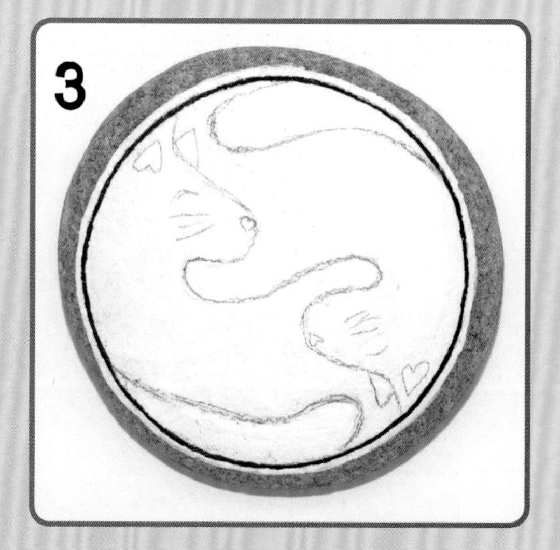

Continue drawing in the rest of the design. Don't forget the whiskers!

Next, use a small brush and black paint to fill in the cat on the right-hand side, and paint the tail at the bottom black, too. Once the paint has dried, use a fine paintbrush and white paint to go over the cat's eye, ear, nose, and whiskers. Paint the white cat's features in black.

When the paint is dry, coat all the white areas with a thin layer of glow paint. Allow this to dry, then repeat the process once or twice more. Allow to dry and coat with protective finish. Now turn off the lights and watch it glow!

Dream Galaxy

Create this unicorn silhouette on a galaxy rock and, when the lights go out, you'll be holding a little piece of magic right in your hands!

YOU WILL NEED:

- Oval-shaped rock
- Paint: black, white, neon pink, neon blue, neon yellow, and glow paint
- Paintbrush
- Pencil
- Masking tape
- Craft knife
- Small sponge
- Toothbrush
- Dotting tool
- Protective finish

Paint the entire top and sides of the rock with a black base coat. Allow this to dry, then add another coat of black paint.

In pencil, draw the outline of a unicorn in the centre of the rock. Use masking tape to cover just the unicorn shape. Ask an adult to help you cut out the tape.

Using the sponge, dab a small amount of white paint across the rock and right over the unicorn outline, blending it so it's blurry.

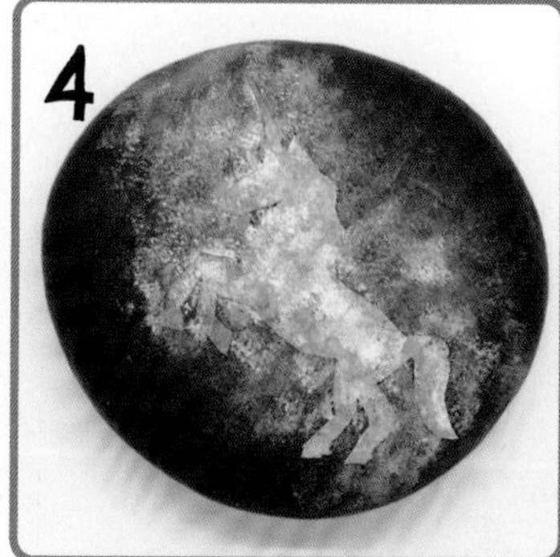

Repeat step 3 using neon pink paint.

Create depth in your galaxy by dabbing a little black paint over the pink and white, to darken it along the sides. When the black paint dries, blur more neon pink over the top.

Use the sponge to add neon blue and neon yellow paint. Dab the blue paint to blend in with the pink for a purple haze, and blend yellow paint into the blue for a hint of green.

Use your glow paint to create stars! Dip the bristles of the toothbrush in glow paint, then run your finger across the bristles to flick tiny bits of glow paint onto the rock. Repeat this with white paint.

Using a paintbrush, add a thin layer of glow paint along the edge of the unicorn outline. When all paint is dry, peel away the masking tape to reveal your unicorn galaxy! Allow to dry and coat with protective finish.

HANDY HINT

When painting with glow paint, turn off the lights every so often, to check how your design looks in the dark.

Isometric Glow

Op-tickle your senses by creating this simple yet mind-bending optical illusion.

YOU WILL NEED:

- Round rock
- Drawing compass
- Pencil
- Ruler
- Paint: white, blue, yellow, and glow paint
- Paintbrushes: small, large
- Protective finish

Using a pencil and compass, draw a circle on your rock. Then, begin to pencil the geometric design, starting by drawing six connected diamond shapes in the centre of the circle.

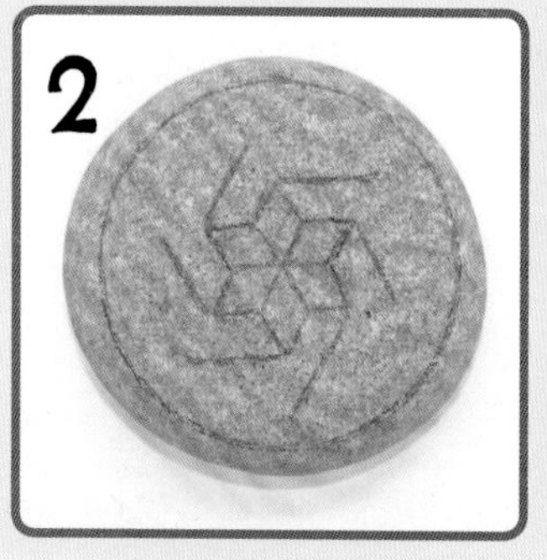

Next, use a ruler to draw a horizontal straight line going from the tip of the upper diamond to the right. Turn the rock and repeat this line for each diamond tip.

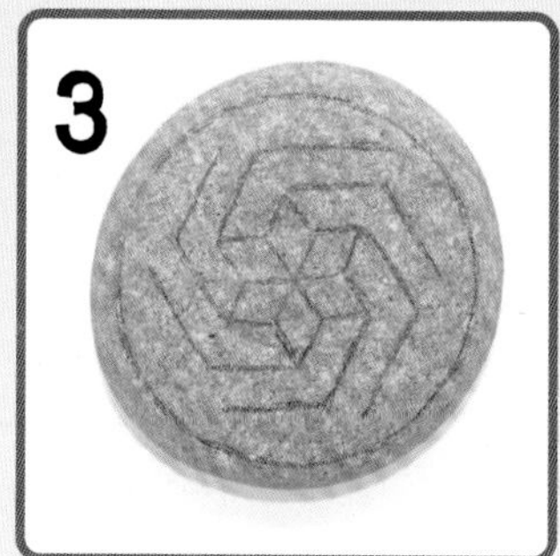

Continue the design by adding another line to each of the lines you made in step 2.

From these lines, draw horizontal lines out to the circle's edge. Fill in the remaining lines as shown, then use a small, thin brush to paint over the pencil lines with white paint. Allow to dry.

Paint the entire circle with a thin coat of white, making sure you can still see your white lines underneath.

Using neon green, blue and yellow paint, fill in the shapes as shown. Try to leave a space between the colours so that the thin white outlines remain. Allow the paint to dry, then add additional coats if needed.

Add one or two coats of glow paint to all the white lines. Turn out the lights and get ready for a geometric glow! Once dry, coat with protective finish.

HANDY HINT

Why not play around with mixing paint to create different shades? You can make colours lighter by adding a little white paint.

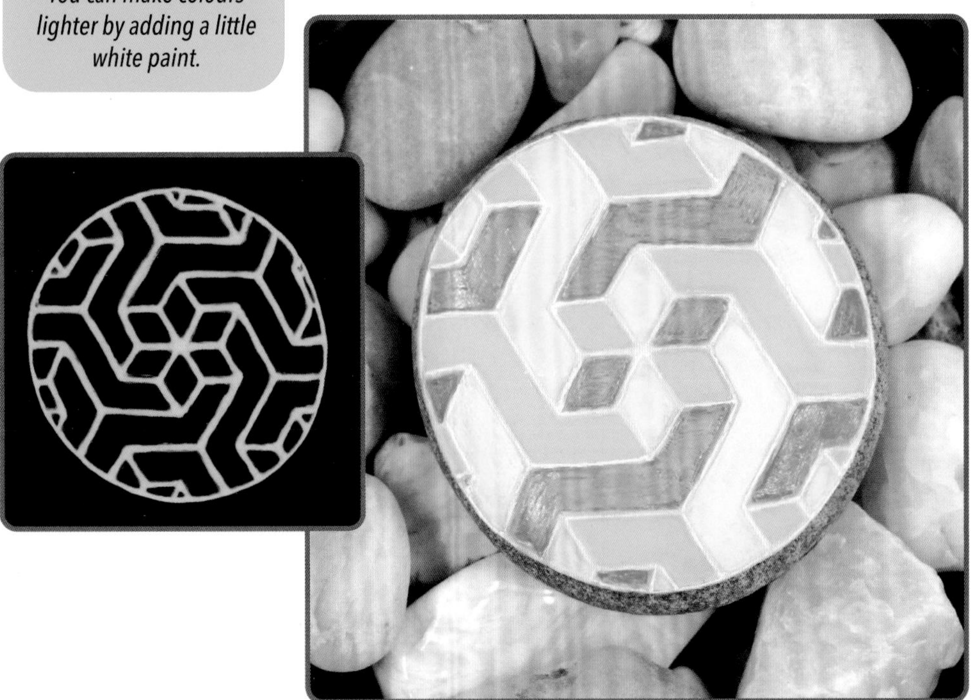

Glow Up

Enjoy all the colours of the rainbow with this layered mandala that shines from the inside out!

YOU WILL NEED:

- Round rock
- Paint: white, light purple, bright blue, blue, bright green, yellow, orange, pink, purple, and glow paint
- Paintbrush
- Dotting tools in a range of sizes from small to large
- Protective finish

Paint the rock with two layers of white base coat and allow to dry. Now add three layers of glow paint, allowing to dry between each coat.

HANDY HINT

With this design, when you fix mistakes, don't forget to make sure the glow coat underneath is still uniform with the rest. Add more glow paint if need be!

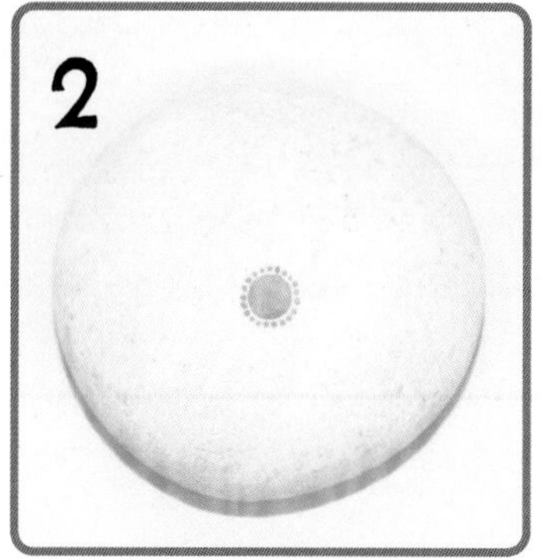

Use a large dotting tool to add a light purple dot to the centre, then surround this with tiny, evenly spaced dots in the same colour.

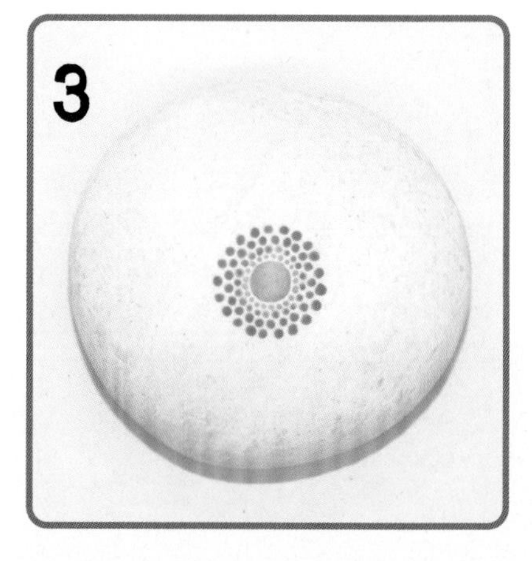

Add the next ring of dots using bright blue paint. Position these dots between each dot of the first ring. Now, continue dotting the entire rock in this alternating dot pattern. As you span out with each new ring, gradually increase the size of the dots.

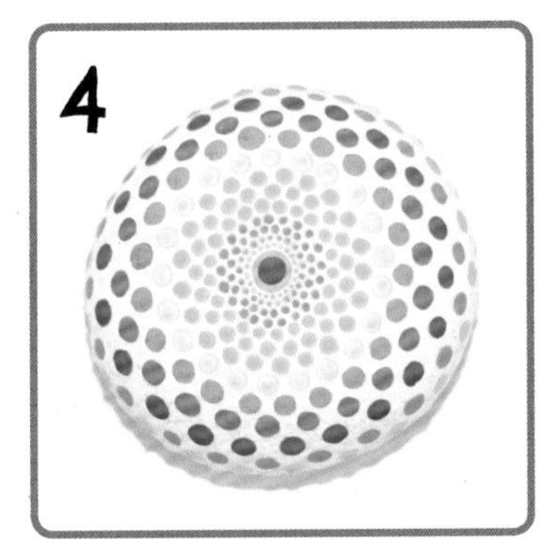

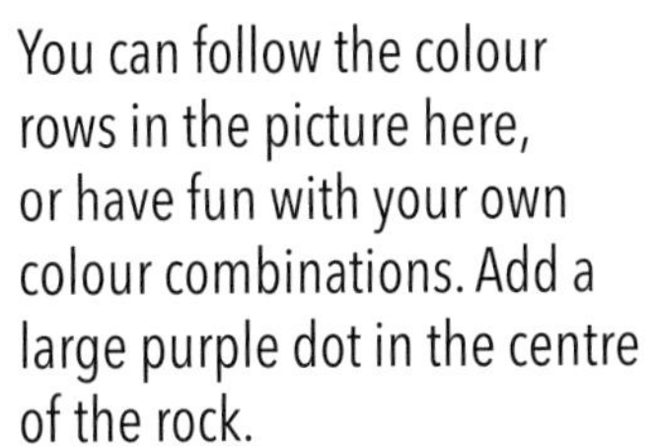

You can follow the colour rows in the picture here, or have fun with your own colour combinations. Add a large purple dot in the centre of the rock.

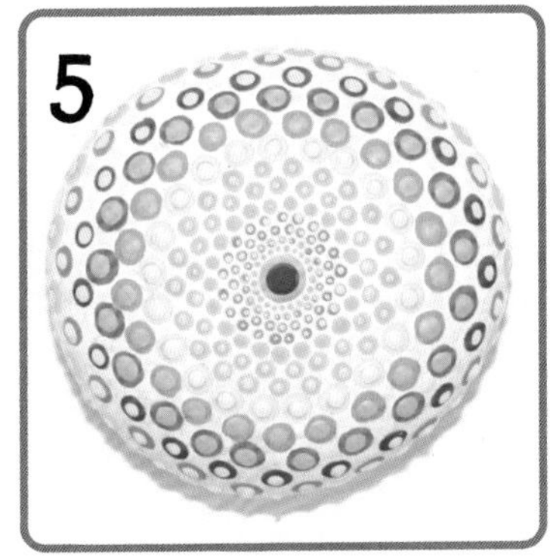

When all the paint has dried, add new dots over each coloured dot in a slightly smaller size, using a lighter shade of the same colour.

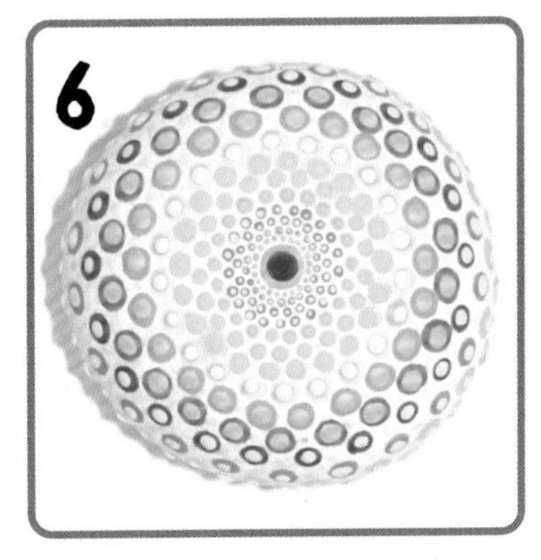

Add a darker dot of purple to the centre dot, inside the lighter purple dot. To finish, add tiny dots of glow paint in the spaces between each of the dots to give you maximum effect when the lights go out! When all the paint is dry, protect your art with one or two coats of protective finish.

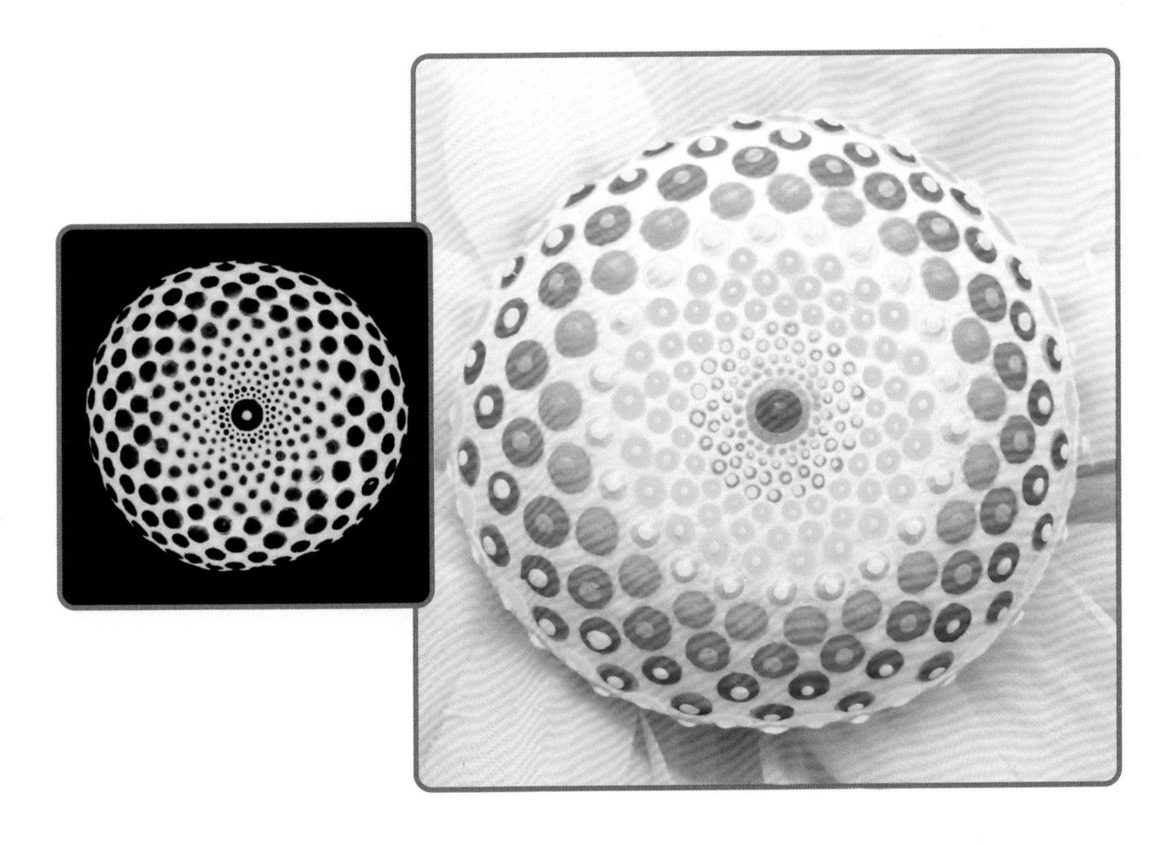

Butterfly

Let your creativity fly! Learn a cool 3D technique and watch the wings of this neon butterfly appear to flutter and flap before your eyes.

YOU WILL NEED:

- Larger rock
- Paper
- Ruler
- Pencil
- Eraser
- Paintbrushes: small, large
- Small liner brush or black paint pen
- Paint: white, black, gray (optional) neon; yellow, pink, orange
- Protective finish
- Torch

HANDY HINT

Find a picture of a real butterfly to copy for your design.

1 Sketch out the design of your butterfly on a piece of paper. If you like, you can measure your rock first to get the sizing just right.

Cut out your butterfly and use it as a stencil to trace your design onto the rock. Paint with a white base coat and allow to dry.

Use a pencil to lightly draw details on the wings, as shown. Try your best to make the two wings match.

Go over the pencil lines with a small brush and black paint or a permanent marker. Fill in the body with black paint and add two lines to the top of the head for the antennae.

Paint the outer edge of the wing cells with neon pink. Dry well between coats of paint to avoid clumping or streaks.

Blend the neon pink with neon orange at the edges of the wings. Painting inward, fill the centre of the wings with neon orange.

Paint the inner part of the wings nearest to the butterfly's body with neon yellow, blending it where it meets the neon orange.

Paint any white speckles around the edge of the wings with neon yellow paint. Add some neon yellow and orange dots on the butterfly's body.

Add grey paint around the edges of the left wing, and at the bottom corner of the right wing. This creates a shadow and a cool 3D effect! Allow to dry then coat with protective finish.

Congratulations!

Well done! Now you've completed these projects, you are the ultimate neon rock star! Think about all the amazing rock-painting techniques you've learnt. You've created intricate line and dot mandalas, drawn and transferred pictures from paper onto rocks, and used sponge-dabbing and paint-flicking to create a swirling, sparkling galaxy! And above all else, you've had lots of practice using neon paint and glow-in-the-dark paint to bring magic and dazzle to your rock art.

Next up, you might like to perfect your dotting skills, creating even more stunning rock mandalas, or try making cute message rocks – they can be cool conversation starters with friends. You could light up a path in your yard so you can see your way at night or create a gorgeous night garden with glow-in-the-dark rocks. What about focusing on themed rocks to celebrate fun events in your family like birthdays or Halloween? The possibilities are only limited by your imagination!